The Moon's Eye

poems by

Sheila Dietz

Finishing Line Press
Georgetown, Kentucky

The Moon's Eye

ACKNOWLEDGMENTS

The Antioch Review: "The Moon's Eye"
The Bluebird Word: "How Light Travels"
Crazyhorse: an earlier version of "Train a Comin'"
Denver Quarterly: "Blue Piping" under the title "Thin Blue Line"
Clare Songbirds Publishing Elizabeth Royal Patton Poetry Prize:
"Foundation Stone," "Close to Nowhere," "Boy on a Bicycle" long listed and
appear in the Anthology.
Clare Songbirds Publishing Elizabeth Royal Patton Poetry Prize 2nd Prize:
"Foundation Stone"
Flipped Mitten Anthology: "The Body's Experience of Religion:" "Parking Lot
Paradise"
Lake Effect: "Battle Lines" won the 1992 Poetry Contest and appeared in the
April Awards Issue
The Massachusetts Review: "Near Black Mesa"
Mid-American Review: an earlier version of "The Murmuring of Fish"
Poetry Miscellany: an earlier version of "Bird Museum" titled "In the Bird
Museum"
In addition, some of the poems in this collection appeared in *The Berry and
The Bee*, published in 2025 by Silverfish Review Press.

Publisher: Leah Huete de Maines
Editor: Christen Kincaid
Cover Art: "The Eye" Photograph by Stephanie Becker
Author Photo: Susan Pszenitzki
Cover Design: Elizabeth Maines McCleavy

Order online: www.finishinglinepress.com
also available on amazon.com

Author inquiries and mail orders:
Finishing Line Press
PO Box 1626
Georgetown, Kentucky 40324
USA

Contents

Amber Past

Drugstore fluorescents spill cold light
across postcards and I spin the rack
that stops again at the image—
a boy in black standing alone,
arms stiff at his sides,
wind stirring sand to blur the horizon
of Coney Island, its futuristic shapes,
stiletto iron spires behind him. Has he turned
his back on their calliope? Who can say why
he stood still for this photograph,
lashed to his own lengthening shadow
sun-draped along rippling sand. Uneasy,

I twirl the rack but he only whirs
past again whispering it is myself
I wish to forget, the girl who drifts like sand
gathering in a doorway. Sand littered
with broken glass recalls my mother's
sequined purse the night I refuse to meet
her martini eyes and say I love you. Or
will I give in again after all? Maybe I won't.
Because I do, but I don't. Toc, toc, toc
go her silver heels, then she pivots,
says "you're not real, you're not even
there," and I'm tied fast in my place by a look
piercing air, unable to save myself from her
palpable wrath. I might as well be the lost one
on this postcard staring at the ground,
unable to erase myself before the camera's
probing eye traps me in an amber past
still audible in hissing grains of sand.

The Embalmers

It rises through the floorboards, seeping
in cracks and spaces around her bedroom
door: formaldehyde. Restless, she courts
sleep but fears worry her awake.

Mom and Dad are at the ceramic table
preserving a four-year-old girl drowned
yesterday. Angry voices ride the vapors
in the white tile room. Dad is drunk.

Rum and coke guide the weaving needle,
but luck finds the vein. He's hidden gin
in the jar marked alcohol, so craving's
stifled. The embalmer's daughter rolls over

onto her back mirroring the body
she envies, the one who keeps her parents
home tonight—why they're still together,
finally quiet, at work. Mom is in charge

of insides; Dad fixes up the eyes
where the peaceful look starts. Tomorrow
her family will say she looks alive.

November Poem

November days grow cold, early darkness
drenching our senses. Thick clouds
remember snow while here, chastened,

we put our hopes in pears
set carefully on the windowsill
to ripen. Nearby, a barn owl yawns.

Bears curl up in dens, slowing their hearts.
They only run now in my dreams
where I know them as anger camouflaged.

Fur shining, muscles rippling, they lumber
between trees, between my decisions.
Do you wonder, as I do, if bears dream us

racing barefoot through these woods
without a path or if they must dream
bear dreams made of berries and trees?

Hush, let us slow our hearts
and see if the mystery will let us in.

The Moon's Eye

(Lyrics quoted from "Shine On, Harvest Moon" by Bayes and Norworth)

Because the moon is a large, marbled button refusing
to hold fast the dark coat of night, I sing "Shine on,
shine on harvest moon," stumble a field with bare

feet numbed by rum, finally tumbling, stubble-cut,
into a silo hooked to an abandoned barn. Squatting,
I smell piss hit corn-packed earth, soak in,

steam fusing with a breath-formed cloud of rum
and smoke, signals aimed at a remote opening of sky.
I want the moon to see me, giddy and daring

like my mother. She'd once gone slumming to ship's
third class with Stew who knew the slickest way
to access the dummy funnel. Empty silo, moon frowning

down. "I ain't had no lovin' since January, February,
June or July." My mother sipped moonshine, smoked
a yellow Gauloises perched on the catwalk spiraling

the funnel wall. She thought trap doors yawned
beneath her feet, but it was only her children, berthed,
who yawned, tossed in a confused sea of dreams,

while snug under plaid blankets, deck chairs listing
with the ship's yaw repeated themselves as if mirrored.
And her husband—where was he? Smoke curls

questions toward a chilled sky whenever I picture her
laughing, kicking up her heels—how she caught the moon's
eye so completely my flung song careens in an empty silo.

Bird Museum

The first day of her job as a librarian
the supervisor hands her a feather duster,
sends her upstairs to dust the birds
arranged behind glass in the 19th century museum
on the third floor of the town public library.
She'd like to refuse but instead is drawn in
by the stuffed eagle and its broken
feathers looking down from a carved wood
tree branch onto the woodpecker
that's flopped over, loose wires curling
from its back. Turning to the house sparrows,
wings folded quietly at their sides,
she sees how their cracked black glass eyes reflect
light as if the sparrows have found a way
to rise above being stuffed, put on display.

One corner of the room features Revolutionary War
cannon balls town residents have found buried in their yards,
and memorabilia a wealthy benefactress brought back
from a trip to China. A bronze soldier's head
perches on a shelf beside some carefully placed
"Indian baskets." The soldier's eyes
are hidden beneath his helmet. It's clear
the artist doesn't expect anyone
to look into smooth, impenetrable
metal. Her feather duster slides

down to the carving on his chest
that says: "Surrender Nothing."

Near Black Mesa

I am the shepherd scanning
brown sand for grass
and I am the lion moving from shadow
to shadow. Both of us
follow the wandering
sheep. Only one of us worries
her back into the fold.
We circle and wait,
circle and wait.

Nothing changes out here.
Rustle of sage,
cadence of lead bell, sheep
talk and clouds.
Goats cause trouble.
Sheep follow anything or play
dead when the dogs get too close.
Grass is scarce.
The sun moves, draining
light from gorges, spilling
color onto hills.
What cannot move disappears
in shade. Lambs are born and wait
in the shadows.
Sooner or later she and I will race
for the lamb knowing
I am the lamb.

When the time comes to move,
the shepherd sits still
too afraid. Surprised.
The lion stretches like a flame
between rocks, burning the lamb to a crisp
in the heat of her mouth.
In the end I am the shepherd longing
to be the lion. I am the lamb
becoming the lion. I am the lion
fading back into the hills.

The Pasture

The edges of this photograph are blurry, the glass
stubbornly dirt-encrusted despite scrubbing.
It's not ours, though left in our basement
atop a tippy stack of old pictures
trapped in wooden frames. The dingy mat's
importantly signed "J. P. Armstrong"
and titled simply "The Pasture"—
just an old, framed photograph of sheep.
Grazing.

Ranged behind them, a grove of trees
turning brown, sepia tones suffusing other
colors. Or maybe it's a murky summer sky
hanging heavily over the farmhouse
barely visible, partly hidden by trees.

Even so, the grass seems cool, crisp beneath
the grazing sheep which have arranged themselves
artistically for J. P., their rounded, wooly backs
curving as they bend their heads to eat.
Three have wandered from the flock
and graze quietly together.
One forages alone.
Except for honeybees buzzing in thistle,
the farmhouse seems quiet. Indoors, the farmer
dozes off reading a tractor manual. A strand of hair
slips from beneath the scarf worn by a woman
kneading bread. Her hands covered in flour,
she puffs air,
it falls back

again. The day has grown warm. The old man
wakes, sticky from afternoon heat building
in his attic room, rolls off the bed, cranks a window
open. He thinks his sons are talking in the barn,
probably about the time two freshly shorn ewes died
shivering in a freak storm. Probably arguing, as they do,

about whose turn it was to bring them in. The farmer
pictures his eldest leaning against a stall.
A horse whinnies, shifts. Some raucous crows
come and go. No one here
calls it murder.

The Murmuring of Fish; Shipwreck 1

The caption reads "mint condition
porcelain awaits recovery," and I count
8 dinner plates from the Nanking Cargo
deep in the South China Sea,
stacked on Geldermalsen's cracked planks—
Dutch merchant vessel sunk on a reef in 1752.

Softened by camera-milked light, dark grains
spill from a teacup. The rest is blurry—
everything out of focus except the goldfish
staring at current-rattled plates,
the downward arc of its mouth sullen
while unblinking eyes widen,
studying these dishes.

That night, I dream a goldfish
swims toward my cuticle, the thumbnail
a thin sheet iced over a fleshy pond,
protective but transparent,
like the glass that covers a framed picture
of my father walking in a field in Spain.
The goldfish tail fans water slowly
as the fish murmurs plates
into my thumb, and I feel unsettled,
amazed by dishes that didn't shatter.

In Madrid, Dad wears a lilac shirt
interrupted by white buttons. He drives
into the country, scoops red poppies
into his arms while we wait
in the car. Just a man who loves flowers, loves to fish—
the same father who baits me with attention,
then feeds tension to feel safe. It's no surprise
that goldfish swim behind my eyes,
want me to recall how I love
the roadside's jagged flash. Broken

bottles jettisoned from cars
and storm-tossed ships, as well
as what survives the wreck intact
attract me, raised as I was to crave
that heady mix of nourishment, neglect.

With Abandon

Once, grasping the horse's mane, I raced
through waves of Juniper, sweet mesquite
the warm afternoon she bolted home

to straw bedding, tail a tangled mass
glistening with sweat destined to be cut,
boiled then woven with cotton, layered

into a mattress. My brother used to rock
himself to sleep on horsehair and straw
that rustled as his body shaped

the torment fueling each arc, kept us awake
with urgent crackling rhythms that eased
and finally lulled him into slumber. Curious,

this cradle embedded habit
that still propelled him back and forth,
back and forth though one day he would push

me away for laughing. I used to walk past
the dusty window of a taxidermy shop because cotton
billowed from the belly of a baby alligator

tipped over onto its side. I'd return to see again
how no one ever lifted it from the display
or sewed it back together.

Train a Comin'

A slack, reddish paw, maybe wild dog or fox
veiled by a crosshatch of bud-thickened twigs

I fingered apart is what I recall this Spring
when my daughter, 10, admits she scouts the forest

ringing the Supply Pond "all the time." Restless,
I'd penetrate a narrow, dense band of woods

bunched between the railroad track, our house,
daily after school, inching deeper with rocks

muddying my denim jacket pocket. Whatever
might need hitting resembled the man who'd pissed

against a concrete wall then left his penis out
so he could watch me stop exploring purple irises,

leaves shaped like swords, not this matted animal
which finally brought a neighbor's missing

Irish Setter to mind, though blurred, a watercolor
left in the rain. Sometimes I'd press an ear to the rail,

strain for a hum—what was coming, so I could center
pennies on the track, jump back into woods until spinning

wheels spit them at me flattened, Lincoln's face
smeared across copper, an "O" gone oval,

though still recognizable as change. I loved
bending that surge of sun-flashing metal to my will,

as if, even as my body, stirring, betrayed me,
I could say what shape a thing would keep or take.

Battle Lines

Afraid the house will catch on fire, you line
the children's shoes up by the door
before you go to bed.
Over the phone, your voice lowers,
"Crazy," you say, and I, silent, agree,
seeing my children's shoes every which way.
On the pad I keep, my red pen draws a sleek car
and I remember you, eleven, walking home alone,
The red car poised beside a hedge, and the man
who tried to draw you in.
Next to the car,
I draw a little girl running.

You tell me you are borderline agoraphobic
and I draw a box around the little girl
whose curly hair I love to spin down the page,
curls like the telephone cord's spiral
I accordion when you ask me to remember
how Mom sent you, eight, back to America
because Grandma, dying of cancer, needed "cheering."
I remember sleeping alone, the vast room
where even the ceiling swelled
with my longing to have been chosen.
"Yes, but think," you say,
"how I felt when she died."
The most wonderful woman
in the world. The one, the family agrees,
you most resemble—her blue eyes,
fighting spirit. I conjure you
dressed for last year's Christmas dinner—
combat pants, T-shirt, even boots. Glaring, you dared
us to say a soldier's clothes weren't perfect.
Drawing parallel lines down the box, I put you
behind bars and wonder what happened to break
rage, make you so afraid.

"I used to be afraid to drive," I offer,
now drawing slanted, neatly spaced lines over the red car.
"And Mom said once she couldn't make herself
turn the corner into town."

Fleshing out the stick legs on my running girl,
I picture burning houses, think how
scattered shoes invite trouble—
lining them up by the door seems wise.

Summer Scene

From a boat on the lake, you see the beach,
a cottage with its red asphalt roof, wicker
chair arranged under big umbrellas. Binoculars

close the distance, pierce the screen's gray blur.
Closer. A woman and a young girl come into focus.
The woman wears a flowered bathing suit, reads

a best seller. The girl, 14, tan legs tucked under
bermudas on the red vinyl chaise, grips a mystery.
But why say "you," when I'm the shocked one

looking back on two people relaxed with books
and morning juice—an outsider, even a friend
might never figure out we're drinking vodka.

I'm on my third. I've only just started my period.
Earlier, cramps for the first time. I'm lucky,
I have the kind of mother you can talk to. She

fixes me a drink to kill the pain, swizzles
something mixed. OJ—Vitamin C, and it goes down
easy. A screwdriver I sip until the waves subside

knowing my mother's sorrow never wavers. Who would
believe her baby brother drowned in a wooden vat,
her sister breathed fumes pumped into the emptied

house, her brother's car crashed on a rain-slick
bridge? Sheer life spared her for every morning
she wakes up without them and grief stirs, wants

attention, gets deadened. By now I feel like velvet,
like swimming to the lighthouse. Leaping up, I ask
for another. "Sure," she says, "help yourself."

Blue Piping

Black lozenge from a distance, with arms, legs
that make it a bear dancing around a driftwood
burning fire. I don't know why. Scared, so I head
straight for my mother's lovely yellow bedroom,

slowed by thick time. The bear floats in the door,
gets close and far away at once. Its wet fur
blocks the sun which should be spilling yellow air
through the window into which all good things pour.

Then my daughter's disembodied head wobbles
into view, floats serenely to the ceiling,
bobbing oddly where her face balloons
distracting the bear from me. Reeling

with satisfaction, I prepare to sacrifice her—
the dream lets me extend this offer, and the bear
shows an interest in consuming my daughter
in my place. Relieved, I see this hairy

creature much more clearly—the deep facial folds,
pear belly and thin arms make her understuffed
and like my mother, peering boldly
into my married life in a photograph

of my wedding. She's wearing the beige silk suit
Dad had made in Hong Kong adding a surprise
to her design— piping edges the jacket
she hates because he added this thin turquoise line.

My Mother's Hair

After you died, I found the envelope,
                    never leave
the lock of your hair curled and tied
                    human hair
with a ribbon. I still haven't cried.
                    out for birds
I didn't want to keep the ribboned hair
                    to build their nests
locked in a box. But how could I
                    throw it away
throw it away. Or give it away.
                    collect
Memories of adding
                    twigs and sticks
your hair to fire made me wonder,
                    songbirds prefer to
maybe songbirds
                    use straw or moss
building nests would choose
                    my mother's hair
human hair to cushion twigs for eggs.
                    might trap birds
When I untied the ribbon, my offering
                    could deposit chemicals
fell into the nest,
                    around their eggs
like a tainted gift
                    poisoning their songs
because you were always
                    trapped in the throat
so distracted. Oh yes,
                    as it happens
I almost forgot all the reasons,
                    birds will leave
I couldn't bring myself
                    your hair alone
to cry, although I tried.

17

Her Grandmother's Ghost

"Closed for the Winter" scrawled on the wind-
rattled sign but she walks the wrack where all day
I've hovered above her, a wraith ghost-knowing

that sometimes she sobs because rain has no arms
to hold her, only separate drops, self-absorbed,
flinging themselves on the ground. She sobs

because trees stubbornly won't curl branches
to enfold her and the pine she dreamt gave birth
to her one night stiffens as she presses

her forehead against rough bark. She sobs
because the mothering ocean pulls back
again and again, only returning

to shore to torture her with illusions
of union. She sobs because, although the ground
supports her, it doesn't really care

if she comes and goes. Her throat swallowing
itself all day remembers me, the grandmother
who died of throat cancer the Christmas

she was twelve. I knew she was real, a girl
with thoughts, with feelings. Not just a story
concocted by her parents, another plot

to bury their hopes in. Floating above, behind
her, I drift and sigh as she reels from day
to day, measuring life by the degree

of affection she receives. Again, I mouth
come to me, but these days my arms diffuse light
and like enveloping fog, afford cold comfort.

Sampler

I select white linen, start with an embroidered hill
to ski down on my vermillion silk skis
stitched to the hilltop

where fear once worked to fasten me. Did I imagine
wolves along the edge of the forest the afternoon
my mother said "Go, you'll have fun"?

A running stitch in charcoal gray and white
works well for wolves, with forest green for trees
drenched in a darkness the wolves call home.

I decide to sew the ski house into the center. I'll choose
invisible thread for the remote figures. A mother
and a father enjoying themselves at the party

can't tell what happens once they've sent me
to the cabin with their old friend. Or can they?
Maybe he will help me overcome my fear

of falling. *Black threads for the curtains he closes,*
dark brown for the suitcase he slams shut
and metallic red for his lips. I'll add

my grandmother, place her in front
of the boxy sampler cabin at the top of the hill
as the only one who figured out what happened.

She died in summer becoming the sound
sand sings when it moves. I use beige thread for sand,
red for the lighthouse I embroider using light

blue for blue mist, yellow for the sweet butter
swirling on hotel silver the morning of her funeral
as bluebirds vanish from a linen sky

pulling threads out as they fly, erasing rain-streaked
windows that seem to say: save the old threads.
You may need them again.

Close to Nowhere; Shipwreck 2

The photo caption reads "Mint condition
porcelain awaits recovery," and I count 8
dinner plates from the Nanking Cargo
deep in the South China Sea, stacked
on Geldermalsen's cracked planks
in this picture of a Dutch merchant vessel
sunk on a reef in 1752.

Water might rattle what wrecked
but stayed intact, while the camera's caught
a goldfish staring at ceramic dinner plates,
the downward arc of its mouth sullen,
as unblinking eyes widen. Down here,

close to nowhere, there is no day or night.
No starlight flickers, no sun prints shadowy
shapes of leaves along the ocean floor,
home to mud and worms. What drifts down,
lands without a sound in this, the deepest place
on earth. Nothing could be deeper,
barring love, barring sorrow.

How Light Travels
For Christina (1956-2017)

In this picture it's Christmas morning
and we're opening presents. Carl, five,
looks away from the camera at Mary
who is out of view. He holds a bag—
red fabric tied at one end
with gold ribbon. I, the oldest,
maybe ten, am trying to pull
a fat gold ribbon from a gift wrapped
in white froth. I wear a shy
smile for the camera
which has caught me in my pajamas—
the red ones with a hole in the heel.

And you, baby sister, your wild,
curly hair catching the light,
cozy in your faded red nightgown
with white buttons, are lifting your face
to the person taking the picture.

One hand is open in your lap,
fingers splayed, and still,
two of its fingers held fast
by the other hand—a nascent
reticence that has not yet reached
your mouth, which, open in a wide smile,
reveals pure joy while the light
in your gold flecked eyes
reflects a gold ornament
dangling from a nearby branch.

Oh, Christina,
how can it be that I did not see you
until just now?

Foundation Stone

Today, out walking, I came across
    a lichen-encrusted foundation stone
        chiseled almost 200 years ago

with letters HD and rough numbers. Once
    a quarried granite setting stone anchoring
        a home, now tossed into a ragged line

of mismatched fieldstones—dislodged remnant of an old
    house, like so many we left behind with one move after
        another, homes I long to reinhabit in my dreams. Nightly

I conjure suitcases, pack up my belongings and leave because
    the new owners of these nocturnal houses won't let me
        stay and I am tossed like this cornerstone, landing

in a memory of my father when he would drive the four of us
    to the nearest woods where he urged us to collect
        rocks he'd later toss into the backyard stream flowing

past our forever home, the one we lived in longest, while these stones
    I pass daily only hope to stop a car that's careened off the road
        into sorrow I can't shake, though one day

I did see a garden snake curled on the flat top of the foundation stone
    warming in sun. And today, I startled a mouse to scurry
        between rocks while a bee nuzzled a pink peony

nestled in clusters of creeping buttercup. I still long to return
    the foundation stone to its true home though I know
        the house anchored

is, like me, scattered and detached even as I can see nearby
    tendrils from twining wisteria
        cast about the air for purchase.

The World Behind the World

The roadside is littered—soggy
cigarette butts, a muddy shoelace,
the snow-pressed fur
of a raccoon I've watched fade
over time as its body melts
into that other world we dream

together. Yesterday I smelled bears
beneath a bridge and held
my breath. I was so close to the dream
where wild animals are me. I am still afraid
of dying but not of being dead. Once

the air around me split open
and I could see inside
the world behind the world
into which we will all go like snow
falls into water before it closed
back up, disappearing
into the world we know
like water turning into snow.

Tokopah Falls

I remember where the trail begins—
a wide, sandy path near the river
not far from the old bridge.
As I reach the first hill,
I look up. The moon rushes
over the cliff rim, then stops
as if caught by the branches
of a dead tree perched on this edge.
At the same time, it looks like a balloon
about to burst. I am holding my breath
when it breaks clear and gives me the path.

I scramble through brush
at the base of the cliff.
This leads to rock and denser forest.
Entering that darkness,
I search for the shaft of light
which falls where the trees were cut.
Then I see the deer—
three does together in the meadow,
their eyes yellow globes
that go out when I lose the moon
behind a cloud. I feel my way
more slowly. Boulders loom,
their enormous dark bearing down
as if to press me back. Behind me,
the sound of hooves on stone
and then a stillness which mingles
with the rush of water. As I turn
this last corner, the moon reappears,
riding Tokopah Falls to earth.
Just as suddenly it is swallowed
by another cloud. Or have I
swallowed it somehow? It's true:
For a moment I feel perfect—
whole and full of light.

Boy on a Bicycle

The boy rides down a dirt road, jumps his bike
over deep ruts worn by lumbering carts

weighted down with winter rye. Air swells
redolent of seaweed, salt, waves hissing

just over the tawny horizon. The boy's
hair riffles as he speeds a stone studded road

into town, past his father who, bending,
grabs a handful of powdery earth so fine

it coats the inside of his nose, his hair.
He frowns as the boy rides by kicking

up dust, calls him back. He has something
to say about cover fields of rye, rain

that won't fall from a cloudless blue stretching
lazily above, with no sense of urgency,

sky that lured the boy from his house and drove
the farmer to walk his land, lower his troubled

gaze into rain barrels. The boy leans forward,
speeds up, heedless of the sea's allure, church bells

pealing, his name in the salty air. Something
propels him down this road, pedaling

steadily past drooping fields of rye, past
wild daisies loosening their petals into the air.

Parking Lot Paradise

We park beside a muddy truck.
My eyes open slowly to a chilly drizzle.
Rest stop parking lot: 95 North,
time for a break, coffee,
maybe an egg and cheese.

Across the thin strip of grass, a man,
facing his car door, shawl draped over his head,
bows repeatedly. But something more stirs
the air around him—a rhythm,
purposeful, spirited. A companion,
his long side locks twisted and curled,
hurries through the rain carrying
drinks in paper cups, hops in the car
while his friend swirls his hands in the air
as if to waft his prayer, sending raindrops
splattering into each other.

A girl, about 11, comes running down the sidewalk,
a younger boy close behind. They wear T-shirts
and shorts in the rain, heavier now, and seem suddenly
to be moving in slow motion, rippling
reflected clouds as they splash through puddles,
laughing and I believe I can see each drop
bounce off the boy's pumping arms,
the girl's knees as they pass us
backing out of our spot. They seem like
angels. I want them to be angels.

En Plein Air

Outside my window, a spider web,
unlike any I've ever seen, recalls 16th century monks
hunting funnel-weaver spiders in the Tyrolean Alps,
patiently scraping up webs, reverently painting saints
with a woodcock pinfeather on a canvas
made of silky layers to hang in a church window.
Gossamer painting, so delicate that one day
Ina Cassirer would write "Figures
seem to float in an opalescent haze."

Beneath the monastery, cobwebs spanned
vaulted spaces, drooped between stone columns
where they languished, too dusty to hold paint.
The monks wanted them freshly spun
unlike the remnant web outside my window
where collapsing strands seem attached
at random making a transparent tapestry,
woven filaments that lift and tilt in a light breeze,
clinging to shingles, the window ledge,
erratic and, ladder-like offering only a few
web-trapped, gauzy wings for saints.

Fishing For Light

Monks climbed worn stone
stairs traveling the same path
to prayer, steeped in silence, darkness,
embracing privation and sacrifice
to become one with God,
the light behind their eyes. Then
Theophilus, a Benedictine,
painted silver compounds on glass.
Light mesmerized, carried stories
through stained glass splashing patches,
shifting colors across the wings of a stone angel,
along the floors and into the darkest corner
of a medieval abbey, through glass
that could glow yellow when fired,
cooled, then be held up for the sun
to shine through an angel's yellow hair
and celestial golden wings. Radiating
divine light, an angel playing a lyre—
musical mosaic contained within
an iron frame. How could artist
monks know then that gold is made
inside exploding stars riding
asteroids to earth? Years

later, a woman, pale, farouche,
her blonde hair falling in waves
to her shoulder blades lights the lamp
in a room enclosed with marooned walls.
A green glass leaf trembles in a glass bowl
when she sweeps the curtains aside,
spilling all that fastens her to this world
out the window, golden light that flows,
streams into the pouring rain. Water
absorbed into the astonished night
air quenches light wavering
through the leaf handmade
from an old bottle someone

mined from the kitchen midden
behind the barn. Indoors, stored bins
of bottlenecks and messy piles
—patterned glass, green and brown
drawers of sea glass, shards
from broken bottles tossed
into the fire or round bottomed
mineral water bottles once used as ballast
in ships crossing from Ireland, jagged
edged bottles now washed up,
their surfaces scratched by sand
offered back to the beach by waves
that ran away before anyone could ask
how glass is made of sand when sand
is made of glass. Sea glass
shines again, swims back into liquid,
pooling like the sea it came from
shaped into light green leaves that stiffen
at a distance from burning beech wood logs.

She rummages through boxes
stuffed with rocks and shells,
cabinets lining walls, drawers of strings
for dots to make a glass fish's eyes smooth
as a deep woods pond on a still day, smooth
as the stone path worn down by monks
doing chores, poring over manuscripts
in silence.

The woman is thinking of turning
one more into a leaf that, lifted
to the horizon appears to hold
a forest or the sea. She will
have to move quickly to capture
the breeze inside a glass leaf,
rippled fish to place carefully

in a bowl beside crazed glass
hearts. It could be
anything, really, this superheated sand
and ash melted, made transparent
but it's still shaped like a fish
becoming a glass angel, wings
swimming in light.

Wing Walker

She walks along the wing to feel alive—
out to the edge, as far as she can go
without falling. Until she feels like sky,
she walks along the wing. To feel alive
she hears the roaring winds arrive,
wants to leave herself behind but knows
she walks along the wing to stay alive—
out to the edge as far as she can. Go

to the edge, she thinks, raise your hands,
breathe. God knows you aren't ready
to be carried on wings, understands
how much you love the edge. Open your hands,
feel the spirit roaring through your plan
to walk out to the edge and remain steady.
Go as far as you can. Raise your hands
and let the wings rock you where you stand.

Sheila Dietz grew up in the Netherlands, attended a Dutch school and began conceiving of the world in literary terms at an early age. Her family moved every 2-3 years, and she experienced all the chaos and dislocation that life entailed. The world she created by writing became her one true and safe home. Sheila has been a Bread Loaf Scholar and has received an Individual Artist Grant from the Connecticut Commission on the Arts. Her work has been nominated for a Pushcart Prize. Numerous poems in *The Moon's Eye* appear in her collection *The Berry and the Bee* which won the 2023 Gerald Cable First Book Award from Silverfish Review Press. She received an MFA from Vermont College. She worked as a librarian at the New Haven Free Public Library for many years before retiring as Head of Reference Services. Sheila is the co-founder of the Salt and Pepper Gospel singers (from New Haven, Connecticut) which is reflected in her work, which is often, though not always, spiritual in nature.

www.ingramcontent.com/pod-product-compliance
Lightning Source LLC
Chambersburg PA
CBHW022054080426
42734CB00009B/1338